SERVING OUR
COUNTRY

U.S. COAST GUARD

by Rachel Grack

AMICUS | AMICUS INK

Amicus High Interest is published by Amicus and Amicus Ink
P.O. Box 1329, Mankato, MN 56002
www.amicuspublishing.us

Library of Congress Cataloging-in-Publication Data
Names: Koestler-Grack, Rachel A., 1973- author.
Title: U.S. Coast Guard / by Rachel Grack.
Description: Mankato, Minnesota : Amicus, [2019] | Series: Serving our country | Includes index. | Audience: Grades K-3.
Identifiers: LCCN 2018002414 (print) | LCCN 2018003008 (ebook) | ISBN 9781681516004 (pdf) | ISBN 9781681515625 (library binding) | ISBN 9781681524009 (pbk.)
Subjects: LCSH: United States. Coast Guard--Juvenile literature.
Classification: LCC VG53 (ebook) | LCC VG53 .K64 2019 (print) | DDC 363.28/60973--dc23
LC record available at https://lccn.loc.gov/2018002414

Photo Credits: Alamy/US Coast Guard Photo cover; Shutterstock/Nikola m background pattern; DVIDS/U.S. Coast Guard photo by Petty Officer 2nd Class Adam Stanton 2, U.S. Coast Guard photo by Petty Officer 1st Class Jamie E. Parsons 5; Alamy/Bob Daemmrich 6; DVIDS/Petty Officer 3rd Class Joshua Nistas 9, USCG photo by PAC Tom Sperduto 10–11; AP/AP Photo/Dario Lopez-Mills 13; Flickr/U.S. Coast Guard photo by Petty Officer 3rd Class Dustin R. Williams 14–15; DVIDS/U.S. Coast Guard photo by Lt. Timothy Bonner/Released 17, U.S. Coast Guard photo by Chief Petty Officer Nick Ameen 18–19, U.S. Coast Guard photo by PO3 Sarah Wilson 20–21; DOD/Coast Guard photo by Petty Officer 3rd Class Eric D. Woodall 22

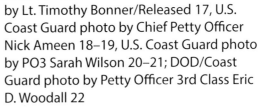

Editor: Wendy Dieker
Designer: Aubrey Harper
Photo Researcher: Holly Young

Printed in China

HC 10 9 8 7 6 5 4 3 2 1
PB 10 9 8 7 6 5 4 3 2 1

TABLE OF CONTENTS

HERE COMES THE COAST GUARD!

Sailors are lost at sea! They signal for help. Who will save them? Here comes the Coast Guard! They help people in trouble on the water.

THE GUARDIANS

The Coast Guard is part of the U.S. **military.** Members are called Coasties or Guardians. They keep ports and waterways safe. They guard oceans, lakes, and rivers.

Force Fact
Guardians save about ten lives each day.

COAST GUARD AT WAR

President George Washington created the Coast Guard in 1790. It was the first armed force on the water. Today, the Coast Guard is part of **Homeland Security**. Guardians protect America from many enemies.

Force Fact
The Coast Guard has served in every U.S. war.

SAVING LIVES

The Coast Guard does **search-and-rescue** missions. A **riptide** pulled swimmers out to sea! Guardians circle above the water in a helicopter. The swimmers are found! Guardians pull them up to safety.

OCEAN PATROL

Someone is bringing illegal drugs across the ocean. Guardians surround the boat and climb on board. The Coast Guard stops the crime!

Force Fact
The Coast Guard patrols more of the Pacific and Atlantic oceans than any other country.

CLEAN WATERS

The Coast Guard protects water environments. A boat is sinking in the harbor! It is leaking oil. Guardians work to stop the spill. They help clean up the water.

WATER ROADS

Waterways have **buoys**. These are like road signs in the water. Boaters count on lighthouses and other markers. Guardians set up and fix these travel aids. The Coast Guard is like the road crew of the water.

ICE BREAKING

The sea is frozen! How will the

ship pass through to Alaska?

The Coast Guard breaks paths

through the ice to **polar** ports.

Heavy **icebreakers** can cut

through 21 feet (6.4 m) of ice!

ALWAYS READY

The motto of the U.S. Coast Guard is "Always ready." Guardians are ready to serve at all times. They work hard to enforce laws, protect Americans, and keep our waters safe.

U.S. COAST GUARD FAST FACTS

Founded: 1790

Members called: Guardians or Coasties

Main duties: Maritime safety, security, and stewardship

Members on active duty: 56,000

Motto: "Semper paratus" (Always ready)

WORDS TO KNOW

buoys A floating marker in a river, lake, or ocean.

Homeland Security A department of the national government that oversees ways to keep the country safe from many kinds of enemies.

icebreakers Heavy ships that break through ice; an icebreaker slides on top of the ice and breaks the ice under its weight.

military Groups of people who work to defend and protect the country; the armed forces.

polar The cold, icy places around the North and South Poles.

riptide A strong sea current that can pull swimmers underwater and away from shore.

search-and-rescue A mission to find stranded people and save them from danger.

LEARN MORE

Books

Mitchell, P. P. *Join the Coast Guard*. New York: Gareth Stevens Publishing, 2018.

Murray, Julie. *U.S. Coast Guard*. Minneapolis.: Abdo, 2015.

Wood, Alix. *Serving in the Coast Guard*. New York: PowerKids Press, 2014.

Websites

Kiddle: Kids Encyclopedia—United States Coast Guard
https://kids.kiddle.co/United_States_Coast_Guard

Learning Lift Off: U.S. Armed Forces
http://www.learningliftoff.com/armed-forces-fun-facts-coloring-pages

INDEX